Compiled
by
Dawn Henry

LMH PUBLISHING LIMITED

Compiled by: Dawn Henry
Edited by: K. Sean Harris
Cover concept by: K. Sean Harris
Cover Design by: Roshane Mullings
Typeset & Book Layout: Roshane Mullings
Illustrations by: Courtney Robinson

Published by: LMH Publishing Ltd.
Suite 10-11, Sagicor Industrial Park
7 Norman Road
Kingston C.S.O., Jamaica
Tel: 876-938-0005
Fax: 876-759-8752
Email: lmhbookpublishing@cwjamaica.com

Website: www.lmhpublishing.com

Printed in China   ISBN: 978-976-8245-92-2

NATIONAL LIBRARY OF JAMAICA CATALOGUING-IN-PUBLICATION
DATA

Names: Henry, Dawn, compiler.
Title: 100 Jamaican sayings / compiled by Dawn Henry |
    illustrations by Courtney Robinson.
Description: Kingston : LMH Publishers, 2020.
Identifiers: ISBN 9789768245922 (pbk).
Subjects: LCSH: Proverbs, Creole – Jamaica. | Creole dialects –
    Jamaica. | Proverbs, Jamaica
Classification: DDC 398.9 -- dc23.

Acknowledgement

To my mother who is always using old Jamaican sayings.

Other titles in the LMH Paperback Cultural Series:

- Learn Fi Chat Jamaican
- The Ganja Dictionary

1.

Yuh see house tan up, yuh nuh know inside.

Translation: You see a house standing, but you do not know inside of it.

Meaning: Until you get to the bottom of a story, it is unwise to draw conclusions.

2.

Money nuh grow pon tree.

Translation: Money does not grow on trees.

Meaning: You have to work hard if you want to achieve success. *(illus.)*

"Money nuh grow pon tree."

3.

Blood tika dan wata.

Translation: Blood is thicker than water.
Meaning: Family comes first. No matter what they may have done to you, at the end of the day they are family.

4.

Monkey see monkey do.

Translation: What a monkey sees it will copy.
Meaning: People are social beings who enjoy copying the habits of others.

5.

Bruk calabash bring new one.

Translation: The breaking of a calabash will bring a new one.
Meaning: Do not waste time dwelling on failed attempts, just try again.

6.

Crab know 'im back nuh trang so 'im nuh dig 'ole.

Translation: Crab knows his back is not strong, so he does not dig a hole.

Meaning: Do not get into situations you know you will not be able to handle, or you will have to bear the consequences.

7.

Dere is no business time caa cure.

Translation: There is no business that time cannot cure.

Meaning: Time is the master of everything and all will fall in place over time.

8.

When bakkle ole rum, cawn 'tick get drunk.

Translation: When a bottle holds rum, corn stick gets drunk.

Meaning: A bad example corrupts everyone, particularly children. *(illus. pg. 5)*

"When bakkle ole rum, cawn 'tick get drunk."

9.

Dog 'ave four foot but caa walk in four way.

Translation: Dogs have four feet but cannot walk in four different directions.

Meaning: There is a limit to what money can do for you. Having a lot of money does not necessarily bring you contentment or happiness.

10.

Dut nuh kill nuh baddy unless it drop pon dem.

Translation: Dirt does not kill anyone unless it falls on them.

Meaning: Don't be afraid to get your hands dirty.

11.

If yuh caa 'ear, yuh wi feel.

Translation: If you cannot hear, you will feel.

Meaning: Failing to heed good advice can lead to dire consequences. *(illus. pg. 7)*

12.

If yuh run too faas yuh run two time.

Translation: If you run too fast you will run twice.

Meaning: If you operate in a hurry you will make costly mistakes. Take time and plan accordingly.

That morning...

Much later that evening...

"If yuh caa 'ear, yuh wi feel."

7

13.

If cow did know how 'im t'roat tan 'im wouldn't swallow seed.

Translation: If a cow knew how its throat was, it would not swallow seed.

Meaning: We should acknowledge our limitations and act accordingly.

14.

Nuh mek yuh left han' know weh de right han' do.

Translation: Do not let your left hand know what the right hand is doing.

Meaning: Keep your secrets to yourself, do not disclose secrets even to those near and dear to you.

15.

Haste mek waste.

Translation: Haste makes waste.

Meaning: Too much rushing can waste time.

16.

Yuh cah hide an' buy lan' but yuh caa wuk pon it inna secret.

Translation: You can hide and buy land, but you cannot work on it in secret.

Meaning: Whatever you cover up, will eventually come to light.

17.

Bline caa lead bline.

Translation: The blind cannot lead the blind.

Meaning: People with similar weakness cannot help each other.

18.

Somet'ing inna somet'ing.

Translation: Something is into something.

Meaning: There is more to this situation than meets the eye.

19.

De only cure fi sleep a sleep.

Translation: The only cure for sleep is to sleep.
Meaning: Irrespective of how busy you are, you must find time to rest and sleep. Nothing can compensate for sleep.

20.

Bush 'ave aise an' wall 'ave yeye.

Translation: Bush have ears and wall have eyes.
Meaning: Be careful of what you say because you never know who is hearing/listening, and news travels fast.

21.

Yuh know weh yuh bawn, but yuh nuh know weh yuh ago berry.

Translation: You know where you were born but you do not know where you will be buried.
Meaning: The path is unknown and the future uncertain.

22.

Dish claat come tun table claat.

Translation: Dish cloth turn tablecloth.
Meaning: Some people who are not accustomed to having expensive things tend to show off when they achieve wealth.

23.

If a nuh suh it go, a nearly suh.

Translation: If it's not exactly so, it is close.
Meaning: There is often some truth in stories you hear on the grapevine.

24.

When fox caa ketch grape 'im seh it sour.

Translation: When a fox cannot reach the grape, he says it is sour.
Meaning: People will speak ill of you, if they cannot control you.

25.

Dawg neva fight ova dry bone.

Translation: Dogs do not fight over dry bones.
Meaning: Do not waste your time on something or
               someone who will not add value to you.

26.

When wata t'row weh it caa pick up.

Translation: When water is spilled it cannot be retrieved.
Meaning: It is no use complaining over something
               that has already gone bad. No use crying
               over spilt milk.

27.

Step like puss pon hot brik.

Translation: Walking like a cat on hot bricks.
Meaning: To walk in a haughty manner. *(illus. pg. 13)*

"Step like puss pon hot brik."

28.
Fowl weh feed a yuh yaad nuh 'ard fi ketch.

Translation: A chicken that is fed at home is not hard to catch.

Meaning: If the places you frequent are known, you will not be hard to find.

29.

Cow read di laws unto dem self.

Translation: Cows read the laws unto themselves.
Meaning: Everyone acts according to the dictates of their conscience.

30.

Count like Jew, gree like bredda.

Translation: Count like Jews, agree like brothers.
Meaning: To be serious in business in spite of friendship or relationship.

31.

When man belly full him bruk pot.

Translation: When a man's belly is full, he will break the pot.
Meaning: A contented man soon forgets where he is coming from or the discomfort and troubles he has experienced in the past.

32.

Nuh pick up bungle weh a nuh fi yuh.

Translation: Do not pick up bundle which is not yours.
Meaning: Mind your own business.

33.

Mistake ongle mek one time.

Translation: A mistake is only made once.
Meaning: Learn from your mistake, so as not to repeat the same error twice. The second time it's not a mistake.

34.

Same way yuh pass mi goin' up di hill, same way yuh pass mi comin' dung.

Translation: The same way you pass me going up the hill, it's the same way you will pass me coming down.
Meaning: Do not forget where you are coming from and always remember to be kind to those you meet on your way up, you might need their help on your way down.

35.

Di more yuh chop breadfruit tree, de more it grow.

Translation: The more you prune a breadfruit tree, the more it grows.

Meaning: Things will always strive under the right conditions.

36.

Pudden caa cook widout fire.

Translation: Pudding cannot cook without fire.

Meaning: In order to do a job efficiently, the right tools are needed.

37.

Man widout a wife is like kitchen widout knife.

Translation: A man without a wife is like a kitchen without a knife.

Meaning: People need companionship. *(illus. pg. 17)*

"Man widout a wife is like kitchen widout knife."

38.

Hard wuk nuh kill nobody.

Translation: Hard work does not kill anyone.
Meaning: Hard work has its rewards.

39.

A promise is a comfat to a fool.

Translation: A promise gladdens the heart of a fool.
Meaning: Do not be swayed by promises.

40.

When kitchen towel tu'n table claat it give knife an' fork heel.

Translation: When a kitchen towel becomes a table-cloth, it gives knife and fork trouble.
Meaning: People who are not accustomed to certain privileges tend to become arrogant when they become privileged.

41.

John crow always t'ink 'im pickney pretty.

Translation: A vulture always think its offspring is beautiful.
Meaning: There is always someone who loves and admires you even with your faults or shortcomings.

42.

If yuh jump outta frying pan yuh jump inna fyah.

Translation: If you jump out of a frying pan, you are bound to drop in the fire.

Meaning: Make sure the situation you are going into is better than the one you are leaving.

43.

When John crow fly too high 'im fedda fall.

Translation: When a John crow flies too high, it loses its feathers.

Meaning: If you act like you are better than every one else, things can happen that will humble you and bring you down to size.

44.

Hat neegle bun tread.

Translation: Hot needles burn thread.

Meaning: Impatience can be disastrous.

45.

If yuh caa walk faas tek time an' run.

Translation: If you cannot walk fast, take time and run.
Meaning: If you cannot find an absolute best solution, use the next best solution available to you.

46.

Nuh ask hungry duck fi watch cawn.

Translation: Do not ask a hungry duck to watch corn.
Meaning: Do not put temptation in people's way. *(illus.)*

"Nuh ask hungry duck fi watch cawn."

47.

Rain nuh fall battam up.

Translation: Rain does not fall from the bottom up.
Meaning: People at the top must set an example for those below to follow.

48.

Yuh caa tan fur an' t'row salt inna pot.

Translation: You cannot stay far and throw salt into a pot.

Meaning: You should not give sensitive information from afar, be discreet.

49.

Di wisest man sometimes tu'n fool.

Translation: The wisest man sometimes does foolish things.

Meaning: Everyone has moments of vulnerability.

50.

Butter cah melt inna 'im mout'.

Translation: Butter can melt in his mouth.

Meaning: Someone overly charming.

51.

If yuh ongle wah half a bread beg somebody buy it, but if yuh wah de ole loaf buy it yuh self.

Translation: If you only want half a loaf of bread, ask someone to buy it. But if you want a full loaf, buy it yourself.

Meaning: The only way to guarantee getting something done to your satisfaction, is to do it yourself.

52.

Haad aise pickney nyam rock stone.

Translation: Hard ears children eat rock stone.

Meaning: Children who do not listen learn the hard way.

53.

Weh 'air nuh deh, nuh put nuh raza deh.

Translation: Where there is no hair, do not put any razor there.

Meaning: Do not go looking for trouble.

54.

If fish coulda keep 'im mout' shet, 'im woulda neva get ketch.

Translation: If fish could keep its mouth shut, it would never be caught.

Meaning: Mind your business and keep out of trouble.

55.

Young bud nuh know when ripe berry deh a mountain.

Translation: Young birds do not know when there are ripe berries on the mountain.

Meaning: There is much to learn from the wisdom and knowledge of older people.

56.

Pig ask 'im muma why 'im mout' so long, muma seh neva mine yuh a grow, yuh wi soon fine out.

Translation: Pig asks its mother why her mouth is so long, mother answers, 'never mind you are growing and will soon find out'.

Meaning: Experience is acquired with time. Experience teaches wisdom.

57.

Wah sweet mout' hat belly.

Translation: What is sweet to the mouth hurts the belly.
Meaning: Some things are not good for you, even though it tastes and looks desirable and it's what you want.

58.

A greed mek fly falla coffin in a 'ole.

Translation: It's greed why flies follow coffin to the grave.
Meaning: Greed can be your downfall.

59.

Yuh t'ink a one day monkey wah wife.

Translation: Do you think monkey wants a wife for only a day?
Meaning: Never forget those who help you today because you may want their help in the future.

60.

Alligetta shouldn't call hag long mout'.

Translation: An alligator should not call a hog, 'long mouth'.

Meaning: Do not point out the flaws of others, while ignoring that you possess the same flaws.

61.

No matter 'ow cockroach drunk 'im nah walk pass fowl yaad.

Translation: No matter how drunk a cockroach is, it will not walk pass a chicken's yard.

Meaning: The natural instincts to protect one's self is strong. One will not knowingly go into harm's way.

62.

Bucket wid 'ole a battam nuh 'ave nuh business a riverside.

Translation: A bucket with holes in the bottom has no business at the riverside.

Meaning: Don't criticise others when you have faults of your own.

63.

*If John crow did know the size a him batty hole,
'im wouldn't swallow pear seed.*

Translation: A John crow knowing the size of its anus,
would not swallow a pear seed.

Meaning: Know your limits and never take on more
than you can handle.

64.

*Nuh matta how a boar hog hide unda sheep skin
'im a go grunt.*

Translation: No matter how a boar hog hides under a
sheep skin, he will grunt.

Meaning: A person's true nature surfaces eventually
no matter how long they pretend to be
who they are not.

65.

Nuh use yuh bare han' an' charm snake.

Translation: Do not use your bare hand to charm a
snake.

Meaning: Do not trouble what doesn't concern
you.

66.

Nuh truble truble, if it nuh truble yuh.

Translation: Do not trouble trouble, if it does not trouble you.

Meaning: Do not do anything to start problems, you might not be able to deal with the consequences. It could backfire.

67.

W'at a gwan bad a mawnin caa come good a evenin'.

Translation: What goes bad in the morning, cannot come good in the evening.

Meaning: A bad situation cannot turn good, you should try something else or another way.

68.

Nuh wait till drum beat before yuh grine yuh axe.

Translation: Don't not wait until the drum beat, before you grind your axe.

Meaning: Be prepared for all eventualities.

69.

Big tree nuh cut dung wid one blow.

Translation: A big tree cannot be cut down with one blow.

Meaning: Perseverance is the key to success. Success takes time. Rome was not built in a day.

70.

Nuh ramp wid mawga cow, it could be bull muma.

Translation: Do not play with a skinny cow, she could be the mother of a bull.

Meaning: Don't underestimate the power of people who seem weak and helpless, you do not know who they are affiliated with, they could have powerful and important connections.

71.

Ask mi nuh question, mi tell yuh no lie.

Translation: Ask me no question and I will tell you no lie.

Meaning: Avoid excessive questions, you might receive incorrect answers.

72.

Nuh be like yuh fren, when yuh caa be like yuh fren.

Translation: Don't be like your friend when you cannot be like your friend.

Meaning: Do not take on more than you can manage, know your limits.
Do not copy others.

73.

A nuh every time rain fall yuh get wet.

Translation: You do not get wet every time it rains.

Meaning: You don't have to be involved in every thing. You should let some things pass you by.

74.

What fit mosquito caa fit elephant.

Translation: What fits a mosquito cannot fit an elephant.

Meaning: Not every style or situation will fit every one. Different strokes for different folks.

75.

Bline man see 'im neighbour fault.

Translation: A blind man sees his neighbour's faults.

Meaning: Too often we are blind to our own short-comings but are quick to point out the short-comings in others.

76.

Nuh tek ugly mek lawf.

Translation: Do not laugh at ugly.

Meaning: One should not mock someone's appearance, weakness or faults.

77.

Before puppy starve 'im nyam cockroach.

Translation: Before a puppy starves he will eat a cock-roach.

Meaning: Use the resources available to you, be flexible.

78.

Nuh swap black dawg fi monkey.

Translation: Do not swap black dog for monkey.
Meaning: Be careful with your choice because you may exchange for something worse than what you presently have.

79.

When man 'ave sintin fi hide, 'im fraid a 'im own shadow.

Translation: When a man has something to hide he is afraid of his own shadow.
Meaning: A man who has something to hide trusts no one, including himself.

80.

Small garden, bitter weed.

Translation: A small garden has bitter weed.
Meaning: Looks can be deceiving, do not always take things at face value. *(illus. pg. 33)*

"Small garden, bitter weed."

81.

If snake bite yuh one time, when yuh see green lizard yuh run.

Translation: If a snake bites you once, when you see a green lizard you will run.

Meaning: Learn from past experience.

82.

Before beard heng long, shave it.

Translation: Before your beard gets long, shave it.

Meaning: Taking care of the situation at hand early will save time and can prevent the situation from spiralling out of control.

83.

Man 'ave raw meat 'im look fi fyah.

Translation: A man who has raw meat seeks fire.

Meaning: It is logical for one to seek solutions to one's problems.

84.

When awse ded, cow get fat.

Translation: When horse dies, cow gets fat.
Meaning: Regardless of how unpleasant a situation is, there is someone who derives benefits.

85.

Scornful dawg nyam dutty pudden.

Translation: Scornful dog eats dirty pudding.
Meaning: It is not wise to be too choosy, sometimes you have to go back to what was rejected.

86.

If yuh nuh mash ants yuh nuh see him gut.

Translation: If you do not mash ants, you do not see his gut.
Meaning: When someone is offended he/she will air pent up grievances.

87.

Dawg caa get cheese 'im get claat.

Translation: When dog can't get cheese, it will eat cloth.

Meaning: Be prepared to accept a substitute when the preferred choice is not available.

88.

Yuh caa sidung pon cow back, an' cuss cow 'kin.

Translation: You can't sit down on the cow's back and curse the cow's skin.

Meaning: You should not abuse the person from whom you are getting benefits.

89.

When cockroach gi party 'im nuh ax fowl.

Translation: When cockroach give party, it does not invite fowl.

Meaning: Be very careful how you mix your friends.

90.

Kanoo weh nuh 'ave good battam, caa go a sea.

Translation: Canoes without good bottoms cannot go to sea.

Meaning: It is foolish to attempt to do something for which one is not properly prepared.

91.

When yuh han' inna lion mout', yuh fi tek time draw eh out.

Translation: When your hand is in a lion's mouth, you have to take your time removing it.

Meaning: Great skill and patience should be exercised in order to get out of a difficult situation.

92.

When dawg 'ave money 'im buy cheese.

Translation: When dog has money, it will buy cheese.

Meaning: When one has money he or she can afford to be self-indulgent.

93.

When ashes cole dawg sleep in deh.

Translation: When ashes are cold, dogs sleep in there.
Meaning: Make the best of an uncomfortable situation.

94.

Puss an' dawg nuh 'ave de same luck.

Translation: Cats and dogs don't have the same luck.
Meaning: Given the same opportunity, no two persons will necessarily come out equal.

95.

Beg wata caa boil cow 'kin.

Translation: Water that is begged cannot boil cow skin.
Meaning: One cannot live off the proceeds of charity.

96.

Nuh every t'ing that 'ave shugga sweet.

Translation: Not everything that has sugar is sweet.
Meaning: One should never judge by appearances.

97.

Bakkle weh nuh 'ave taper belangs to cockroach.

Translation: A bottle without taper belongs to cockroach.

Meaning: Guard your possession or it could become
common property or contaminated.

98.

Quattie buy truble, 'undred pown caa pay fi it.

Translation: Quattie buy trouble, hundred pounds
cannot pay for it.

Meaning: Great troubles many times are caused
from simple issues.

99.

Cock mout' kill cock.

Translation: Cock mouth kill cock.

Meaning: To implicate one's self with careless
chatter.

100.

When man lib well 'im go a pastcha go tell cow how-de-do.

Translation: When man lives well he goes to pasture to tell cow howdy.

Meaning: The devil finds work for idle hands.

Brawta

Meaning: Something extra; bonus.

Nuh draw mi tongue.

Translation: Don't draw my tongue.
Meaning: Don't provoke one to quarrel.

A wink is as good as a nod to a bline man.

Translation: A wink is as good as a nod to a blind man.
Meaning: An intelligent person needs only the slightest hint to understand when his/her behaviour is out of line.

Chief in town, ginal mus 'lib.

Translation: Idiots in town, smart- alecs must live.
Meaning: As long as there are fools, there will always be unscrupulous persons to take advantage.

Mi yeye a mi market an' yuh a mi coco basket.

Translation: My eyes are my market and you are my coco basket.
Meaning: I look wherever I please.

Wile de grass a grow de horse a starve.

Translation: While the grass is growing the horse is starving.

Meaning: Although the future looks bright the present is not good.

Weh de horse tie, a deh 'im nyam grass.

Translation: Where the horse is tied, that is where he eats grass.

Meaning: A man must eke out an existence wherever he finds himself.

Puss nuh business inna dawg fight.

Translation: Cat has no business in dog fight.

Meaning: Do not get involved in what is not your affair and is of no concern to you.

Rock stone a riva battam nuh know sun hat.

Translation: Rock stone at river bottom does not know the sun is hot.

Meaning: Those of the privileged class do not experience hard times.

Ebery lickle mickle mek a muckle.

Translation: Every little mickle makes a muckle.
Meaning: Every little contribution is of significance.

Howdy and tenky nuh bruk nuh square.

Translation: How-de-do and thank you break no square.
Meaning: It does not cost you to have good manners and be polite.

When bull ole, yuh tek plantain trash fi tie 'im.

Translation: When bull is old you take plantain trash to tie him.
Meaning: More often than not, humiliation comes with age.

Yuh cah get 'ouse, yuh affi tan unda cow belly fi save mawnin dew.

Translation: You can't get house, you have to stand under cow belly to save morning dew.
Meaning: One should learn to make the best of his/her present situation.

Fisherman nebba say 'im fish 'tink.

Translation: Fisherman never says his fish is stink.
Meaning: A sales person never points out the fault of the commodity he is selling.

Jackass weh gallop an' kick muss get cucoo macca 'tick.

Translation: Donkey that gallops and kicks must get cucoo macca stick.
Meaning: One who misbehaves or does wrong must be punished.

A nuh fi di want a tongue mek cow no talk.

Translation: It is not for the want of a tongue why cow does not talk.
Meaning: It is not necessarily for the want of power why someone does not speak or act.

Silent riva run deep.

Translation: Silent river runs deep.
Meaning: Do not underestimate a quiet person. A quiet person should not be taken for a fool.

Crab walk too much 'im lose 'im claw. 'im nuh walk 'im nuh fat.

Translation: Crab walks too much he loses his claw. If he does not walk he does not get fat.
Meaning: While it is risky to be too adventurous it is also unrewarding to be too cautious.

One one coco full basket.

Translation: One one coco full basket.
Meaning: It is not the size but the consistency of the contribution that matters.

Yuh ketch cow by 'im awn, but man by 'im wud.

Translation: You catch cow by their horns, but men by their words.
Meaning: Be careful of your words because once spoken they cannot be taken back and could have a devastating lasting effect.

Nuh dash weh yuh 'tick before yuh dun cross ova.

Translation: Do not throw away your stick before you have finished crossing.
Meaning: Do not be ungrateful, because another favour may be needed.

Like how washa ooman look pon dutty clothes pon Monday morning.

Translation: Like how washer woman looks on dirty clothes on Monday mornings.
Meaning: Looked at in a disdainful manner.

Cow seh tan up nuh mean res'.

Translation: Cow says standing up does not mean rest.
Meaning: Cow is a cud-chewing animal so it is working even while standing still, so never be taken by appearance.

If yuh nuh go a man fiah side yuh nuh know 'ow much fiah 'tick bwile in pot.

Translation: If you do not go to man's fire side you will not know how many firestick boil his pot.
Meaning: You can only know someone's personal affairs by getting close.